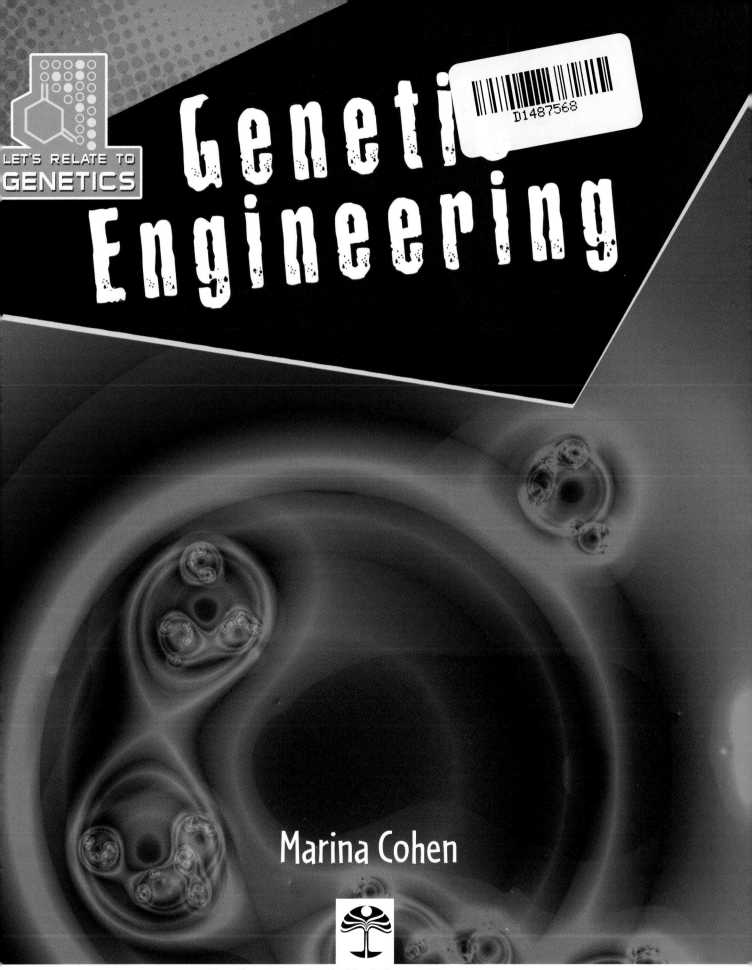

LET'S RELATE TO
GENETICS

Genetic Engineering

Marina Cohen

Crabtree Publishing Company

www.crabtreebooks.com

Crabtree Publishing Company

www.crabtreebooks.com

Author: Marina Cohen
Coordinating editor: Chester Fisher
Series editor: Jessica Cohn
Editorial director: Kathy Middleton
Editor: Adrianna Morganelli
Production coordinator: Katherine Berti
Prepress technician: Katherine Berti
Project manager: Kumar Kunal (Q2AMEDIA)
Art direction: Harleen Mehta (Q2AMEDIA)
Cover design: Tarang Saggar (Q2AMEDIA)
Design: Supriya Manna (Q2AMEDIA)
Photo research: Mariea Janet (Q2AMEDIA)

Photographs:
123RF: p. 9
Associated Press: Winfried Rothermel: p. 20
Canstockphoto: Marcopolo: p. 11 (top)
Capital Pictures: p. 24, 33 (top)
Dreamstime: Byron Moore: p. 4
Getty Images: David S. Holloway: p. 38-39
Istockphoto: Warwick Lister-Kaye: p. 5 (right); Stan Rohrer: p. 7 (left);
    Leigh Schindler: p. 7 (right); Chris Rogers: p. 12; Bershadskyy Yuriy:
    p. 13 (bottom); Chris Rogers: p. 17 (top); Sharon Dominick: p. 19;
    Foto Pfluegl: p. 23 (top); Yulia Saponova: p. 31; Floris Slooff: p. 35 (left);
    Jan Tyler: p. 39; Rachel L. Sellers: p. 40
Life Sciences Division, Oak Ridge National Laboratory; U.S. Department
    of Energy Human Genome Program: Mitch Doktycz: p. 33 (bottom)
Photolibrary: Vem: p. 17 (bottom), 18 (top); Cavallini James: p. 18 (bottom)
Reuters: Jeff J Mitchell UK: . 23 (bottom); Ho New: p. 43 (bottom)
Shutterstock: Norman Chan: cover; Gina Sanders: cover; Benjaminet: cover;
    Spbphoto: p. 1; Joseph Calev: p. 5 (left); Gautier Willaume: p. 6;
    Liale M: p. 8; Sensay: p. 11 (bottom); Sebastian Kaulitzki: p. 13 (top);
    Einstein: p. 16; Arvind Balaraman: p. 21 (top); Plampy: p. 21 (bottom);
    Spbphoto: p. 22; Hywit Dimyadi: p. 25; Gravicapa: p. 26; Tree of Life:
    p. 28; Lessadar: p. 29 (top); Baloncici: p. 29 (bottom); Elaine Hudson:
    p. 32; Tatiana Popova: p. 34; Raia: p. 35 (right); Inacio Pires: p. 36-37;
    Valio: p. 37; Motionstream: p. 41; Ana Blazic: p. 42; Lezh: p. 43 (top);
    Ultimathule: p. 43 (top); Gilmanshin: p. 43 (top); Olga Lyubkina: p. 43
    (top); Sjoerd van der Wal: p. 43 (top); Jeff J Mitchell UK/Reuters: p. 45
Q2AMedia Art Bank: p. 10, 14-15, 44
Q2AMedia Image Bank: p. 30
Yorktown Technologies: 2006 Yorktown Technologies, L.P. ("Yorktown"):
    cover, p. 27

Cover:
Main image:
    The double helix of DNA
Inset images:
    The enviropig is genetically modified to produce about 75
    percent less phosphorus in its manure than typical pigs. This
    is better for the environment. Scientists are working on trying
    to "silence," or shut off, the gene in the peanut that causes an
    allergic reaction. Will science be able to revive the dinosaur
    using genes from fossils, as they did in the Jurassic Park movies?
Can we improve on nature?:
    This is a hotly-debated question. Can we, and should we, use
    what we know about the science of living things to improve
    our quality of life? On one side, there are unimaginable benefits,
    such as eliminating debilitating diseases; on the other side lies
    the potential for risks that we have no way of foreseeing.

Library and Archives Canada Cataloguing in Publication

Cohen, Marina
    Genetic engineering / Marina Cohen.

(Let's relate to genetics)
Includes index.
ISBN 978-0-7787-4950-9 (bound).--ISBN 978-0-7787-4967-7 (pbk.)

    1. Genetic engineering--Juvenile literature. I. Title. II. Series: Let's relate
to genetics

QH442.C64 2009   j660.6'5   C2009-903885-4

Library of Congress Cataloging-in-Publication Data

Cohen, Marina.
    Genetic engineering / Marina Cohen.
        p. cm. -- (Let's relate to genetics)
    Includes index.
    ISBN 978-0-7787-4950-9 (reinforced lib. bdg. : alk. paper)
    -- ISBN 978-0-7787-4967-7 (pbk. : alk. paper)
    1. Genetic engineering--Juvenile literature. I. Title.
    QH442.C644 2010
    660.6'5--dc22
                                        2009024759

Crabtree Publishing Company

www.crabtreebooks.com   1-800-387-7650

Printed in the U.S.A./092014/CJ20140801

Published in Canada
Crabtree Publishing
616 Welland Ave.
St. Catharines, ON
L2M 5V6

Published in the United States
Crabtree Publishing
PMB 59051
350 Fifth Avenue, 59th Floor
New York, New York 10118

Published in the United Kingdom
Crabtree Publishing
Maritime House
Basin Road North, Hove
BN41 1WR

Published in Australia
Crabtree Publishing
3 Charles Street
Coburg North
VIC, 3058

Contents

Chapter 1

Genetic Engineering

What do you get when you cross a chicken with a centipede? You get drumsticks for everyone. How about a vampire with a snowman? Frostbite! A dinosaur with a termite? That would be "dino-mite."

Okay, stop groaning. Let's consider the possibility of crossing unlikely pairs in a serious way. What if crossing a pig with a worm made the pig's fat more like the worm's body--and bacon more healthful? How about crossing a spider and a goat to make a goat that produces silk?

Welcome to the wonderful and sometimes weird world of **genetic engineering**. **Genes** are the chemical codes that determine how living things look and act. Tinkering with that code is the basis of genetic engineering. Sometimes genetic engineers simply remove a piece of chemical information. Sometimes they might transfer information from one living thing to another. By making slight changes in organisms, scientists hope to cure serious diseases. Researchers may even help end world hunger by producing stronger plants and healthier animals.

Imagine using genes from fossils to revive dinosaurs.

In the Lab

The genes that allow termites to digest wood might also help humans.

Like One Big Family

About six billion humans live on Earth. About 99 percent are genetically identical. That may be hard to believe. You may think you look nothing like your neighbor. Yet if you compare yourself to a butterfly for example, it is easier to think about the many things that you and your neighbor have in common.

How does genetic engineering work? What are some of its benefits? What are some of the dangers of experimenting with living things? Come explore the world of genetic engineering. Discover how imagination and science have made some incredible—and sometimes frightening—things happen.

Chapter 2

Discovering Genes

Changes in living things have always happened naturally. When did science jump in and start mixing things up?

Natural selection is nature's own brand of genetic engineering. Environments are constantly changing. The living things that are best able to adapt to these changes do well. They survive and pass on their genetic information to the next generation. This natural way of the world is also known as "survival of the fittest." A scientist named Charles Darwin made these ideas well known.

Long before Darwin, farmers were using genetics. Farmers chose seeds from only the best plants. Only the strongest or largest animals were chosen for breeding. This process is known as **selective breeding**. Selective breeding is an early form of genetic engineering.

Some of the earliest genetic engineering happened on farms.

Using pea plants, Gregor Mendel proved that traits were passed down.

Designer Dogs
Why do we **crossbreed** canines? We do this to strengthen certain traits. For example, some people are allergic to dog hair. Crossbreeding creates dogs that do not cause people to sneeze. Crossbreeding can also reduce a dog's inherited disorders. It can also create novelty dogs. You can own a schnoodle, a chiweenie, a German Chusky, a cockapoo, a labradoodle, or a moodle.

Pass the Peas

For thousands of years, people understood that they got certain traits from their parents. Until Gregor Mendel, people believed that a child's traits were a simple combination of traits from both of his or her parents. Mendel proved this wrong. In his experiments, he crossed smooth, yellow pea plants with wrinkly, green pea plants. The first set of offspring was yellow and smooth. In the second generation, however, some green and wrinkly peas grew. In this manner, Mendel proved that certain traits are **dominant** while others are **recessive**. His experiments paved the way for modern genetics.

Fast Forward

The results of Mendel's experiments were published in 1866. Yet it wasn't until 1900 that researchers understood how important his findings were. Many more years passed before the beginning of what we call modern genetics.

1909—Wilhelm Johannsen uses the word *gene* for the first time

1913—William Bateson uses the word *genetics* for the first time

1953—James Watson and Francis Crick discover the structure of **deoxyribonucleic acid**, or **DNA**, the chemical code that carries genetic information

1967—copies of mice are produced by Japanese and American scientists, using DNA

1973—DNA is cut into pieces, rejoined with other DNA, and put back into **bacteria**

1982—DNA is transferred from one type of fruit fly to another; the first genetically engineered drug is approved for sale

1986—the first field test of genetically engineered plants is undertaken

1987—a gene from a bacterial **cell** is put into a tomato plant, making it resistant to caterpillars

The first plants to be genetically engineered were tobacco plants.

Scientists are studying the genome of chimps.

1988—genetically engineered mice are
produced for cancer research
1990—**Human Genome Project**, an attempt
to map out all the DNA in humans,
officially begins
1992—the first genetically engineered food
product is approved for consumers—
a tomato genetically engineered to stay
firmer longer
1996—Scottish scientists successfully make
a copy of a sheep from the cells of an
adult animal
2000—130 countries agree to identify all
genetically engineered crops on
product labels
2003—Human Genome Project is completed
2005—chimpanzee genome studied
2006—an attempt to map cancer begins
2009—a new technique is announced for
studying the human genome

In the Lab

Predicting the Future
As early as 1896, writer
H.G. Wells predicted
the modern world of
genetic engineering in his
science-fiction classic
The Island of Dr. Moreau.
Wells's bone-chilling novel
is about a mad scientist
who experiments with
crossing animals and humans.
The results are horrific.

Chapter 3

DNA at Work

If life were a book, the story would pretty much begin with cells. Cells are the tiny building blocks of which every living thing on this planet is made.

To understand how scientists are able to take information from one plant or animal and put it into another, we first need to take a closer look at the cell. There are two basic types to consider.

Plants and animals are made up of **eukaryotic cells**. Plant and animal cells have a small, round compartment inside. The compartment is called a **nucleus**. The nucleus contains, among other things, the cell's **chromosomes**.

Chromosomes are tiny beaded threads made of **proteins**. Chromosomes carry the cell's genetic material, known as DNA. A typical human cell has 23 pairs of chromosomes—a total of 46.

DNA looks like a spiral ladder or staircase. The information stored in your DNA works like a set of instructions. These instructions tell the cell which proteins to make. Proteins are what give each cell its form and its specific job.

nucleus

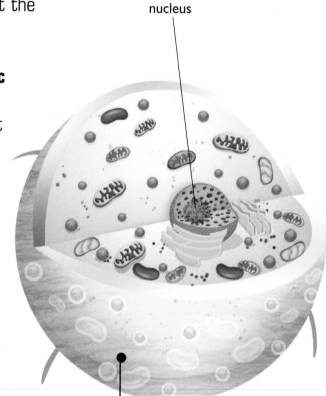

The main compartment within a eukaryotic cell is the nucleus.

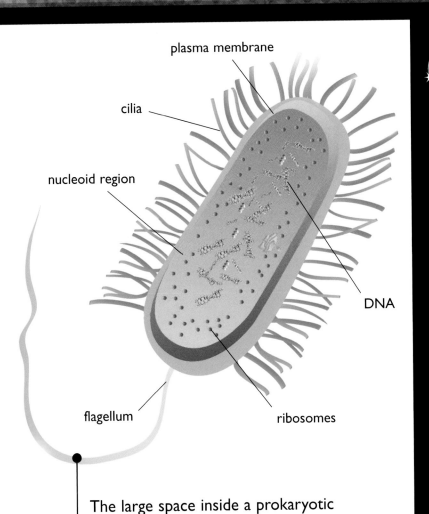

plasma membrane

cilia

nucleoid region

flagellum

DNA

ribosomes

The large space inside a prokaryotic cell is called a nucleoid.

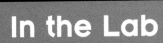

If DNA Were a Book
Your DNA book would be over one billion words long. It would need three gigabytes of computer storage space. Yet all this information fits neatly into the cell's nucleus. The nucleus is the size of the point of a pin!

DNA also decides what a living thing looks like. Your DNA says if you will be short or tall. It decides whether you have green, blue, or brown eyes.

The second kind of cell is found mainly in bacteria. **Prokaryotic cells** have a large space inside them. The space is called a **nucleoid**. The genetic material in prokaryotic cells is contained in one large circular chromosome and in smaller circular structures.

11

Bases and Staircases

The DNA in each chromosome is like a long spiral staircase, or ladder. This staircase is made up of 50 million to 250 million steps. The steps are made of chemicals called **bases**. There are four bases: **adenine**, **thymine**, **cytosine**, and **guanine**. Each individual step is a combination of two of these four bases.

Each section of steps along the DNA staircase is a gene. A single gene gives the cell instructions to make one kind of protein. Human DNA carries the instructions to make over 100,000 different proteins. Each protein has an important job to do.

The average human gene has about 3,000 steps. If one gene is like one flight of steps, think of all your genes put together. That number of steps would lead up a tremendously tall skyscraper.

A butterfly has its own genome.

12

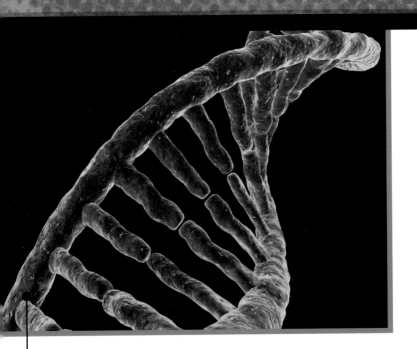

If you could view DNA it would resemble this twisted ladder.

Compare and Contrast
Yeast has approximately 6,000 genes. Humans have approximately 30,000. Humans have 46 chromosomes. Orangutans have 44, and butterflies have 380! A mosquito has six chromosomes, while corn has 20.

Your Very Own Genome

The entire collection of DNA that makes up a living thing is known as its genome. Each living thing has a genome. There is a human genome. There are different genomes for a butterfly, a tiger, or a stalk of corn.

Scientists have long wanted to map the human genome. Figuring out which two chemicals make up each step of DNA would be like seeing the blueprints of human life. Knowing which two chemicals make up each step and the order of steps would allow scientists to jump in and make changes. Could they use what they learned to cure serious genetic diseases? That is exactly what they have done! The Human Genome Project was officially launched in 1990. It was supposed to take 15 years, but work was completed in 2003, two years ahead of schedule. Some work still needs to be done, but researchers have sketched out the genome of human life.

13

Take a Closer Look

Eukaryotic Cell

All multicellular organisms are made up of eukaryotic cells. The larger central structure of eukaryotic cells is the nucleus. Most of the cell's genetic material is housed in the nucleus.

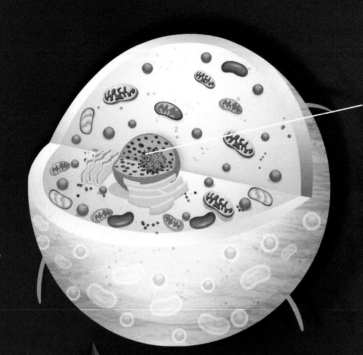

nucleus

Nucleus

The nucleus is like the cell's brain. It controls what the cell looks like and what it does. The nucleus contains the cell's chromosomes.

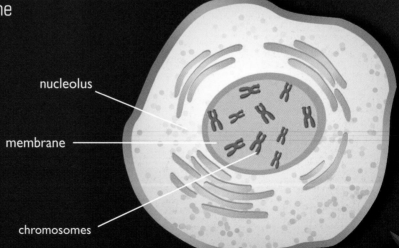

nucleolus

membrane

chromosomes

DNA

DNA is about 1,000 times the length of the cell, so it must twist and fold into itself to fit inside the nucleus. By making changes in DNA, scientists are able to make changes to the cell. This is what genetic engineering is all about.

bases

Chromosome

Chromosomes are made up of tightly coiled DNA.

DNA coil

A Walk on the Wild Side

Chemists have created a DNA bipedal walker. What is that? It is defined by what it can do. It can move independently along the tracks of DNA. The walker imitates kinesin. Kinesin is a protein that moves things from one place to another place in a cell. The walker moves along a track of DNA strands, powered by chemical changes between the walker and the track. The length of the track is 49 nanometers long. A nanometer is one billionth of a meter. The creation of the walker is a step toward making more complicated artificial systems.

A Little of This and That

How does genetic engineering work? One way is by causing cells to copy themselves. The cells carry DNA, and DNA is responsible for telling the cell what proteins to make. Cells can reproduce naturally by making copies of their DNA and then dividing into two. Since the 1970s, researchers have been able to start up the copying process in laboratories. This method is called **recombinant DNA**. It works this way. Scientists:

1. locate a specific gene
2. cut out the section of DNA that carries that gene
3. cut out a section of DNA in a **plasmid**, creating a gap
4. insert the gene into the gap in the plasmid
5. insert the plasmid into a cell
6. let the plasmid multiply
7. allow the cell to grow and divide
8. new cells use the information from the new gene to make new proteins

Insulin for people with diabetes used to be taken from pigs and cows. Now recombinant DNA is used to make insulin.

Insulin Factories

The cell can be tricked into producing proteins it normally would not make if foreign DNA is added. For example, diabetes is a serious, sometimes life-threatening disease. Diabetics aren't able to produce enough insulin. Insulin is responsible for breaking down sugar in our bodies. In the past, people who needed insulin got it from cows and pigs, but there were risks involved. If the animal was sick it could pass on its illness in the insulin. In 1982, scientists developed a new, risk-free way to make insulin. By placing human DNA inside bacteria cells, scientists tricked the bacteria into making human insulin.

Bacteria cells such as these (*Streptococcus pyogenes*) typically start an infection on the skin or in the throat.

Special Delivery

Viruses are little pieces of DNA dressed up in protein coats. They cannot survive on their own. In order to stay alive, viruses use their protein coats as a sharp edge. They pierce their way into cells and take control. Viruses use the cell's parts to reproduce themselves and spread. Normally, this is not a good thing. Having a virus invade your cells can cause you to become sick. Scientists have figured out a way to make viruses work in their favor, though.

First, scientists take out the genes in the virus that make living things sick. Next, using the steps in recombinant DNA, the scientists attach new pieces of DNA to those of the virus. Then, the scientists let the viruses loose on the target cells.

Viruses are structured with sharp edges, as this diagram shows.

Here, you can see the HIV virus at work, attacking a cell.

The viruses do their thing. They invade the target cells, and they carry the good DNA into the cells. The viruses "think" the good DNA is their own.

The process comes with risks. For one thing, a virus sent into a human body may infect healthy cells along with sick cells. Another problem can occur if the virus inserts the new DNA into the wrong spot. This can cause severe **mutations**.

Delivering genes into humans and animals is tricky. Yet this method is so promising that scientists continue to work hard at fixing the potential problems.

In the Lab

Ill Treatment
Vaccines are made by giving people weak or dead versions of a virus so the body learns to fight off that virus. A virus called swine flu appeared in 1918. To make swine flu vaccine, scientists looked for volunteers at a prison. Prisoners were promised they would be released if they survived. They were sprayed in the eyes, nose, and mouth and even injected with germs. They had their throats swabbed with infected mucus. Sick people coughed at them. Not one single prisoner got sick! The only person who became ill and died was the prison doctor.

Cold viruses attach themselves to cells at the back of the nose.

19

Ready, Aim, Fire

Laboratories have taken a cue from shooting ranges. In 1987, scientist John Sanford developed a gene gun that shoots DNA into plant cells. This process is called **biolistics**. It was first tested on onions at Cornell University in New York. The bullets used in the gene gun are made of heavy metals such as tungsten, silver, and gold. Yet they are tiny. The bullets are one billionth of a meter in diameter.

Scientists can attach DNA to the bullets and then fire at target cells. A shield stops the shell cartridge, but tiny holes in the shield allow bits of metal through. The bits of metal pass into the living cells, carrying foreign DNA with them. Researchers can also fire uncoated metal particles at the target through a solution containing DNA. In either case, the cells are tested afterward. Those that carry the new DNA are encouraged to grow.

A gene gun shoots bullets that carry DNA.

The exterior layer of a cell is called the **plasma membrane**. It is tough, but the membrane allows things to pass through it. Plant cells have another outer layer called a **cell wall**. The cell wall is even harder. Yet biolistics can blast new DNA through the cell wall right into the nucleus of the cell. The new genes can make the plants resistant to insects. New genes can also help plants stand up to the bug sprays that keep away pests. Crops that have been improved using biolistics include rice, wheat, soybean, tobacco, and corn.

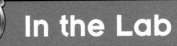

In the Lab

Golden Rice
Scientists have added genes from daffodils to rice. This turns the rice a lovely shade of gold. It also makes the rice much higher in vitamin A. The new rice is not available for sale yet, but it shows what good things can be done.

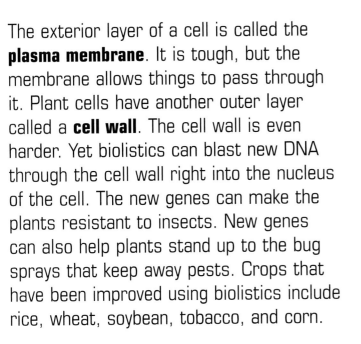

Wheat is one of the crops that biolistics has improved.

Send in the Clones

The mention of the word **clone** makes some people think of humanoid armies from science fiction, in which all the soldiers look the same. Other people think of alien plant pods that grow people. We get these ideas from scary movies. Let's set the cloning record straight.

Identical twins and other multiples are actually natural clones. When something is cloned, its DNA has not been changed. The Food and Drug Administration (FDA) considers cloned animals less radical than those that have been genetically modified.

Genetic information is contained in a cell's nucleus. In cloning, you take the nucleus from an egg cell and replace it with the nucleus of an adult cell. The **embryo** is implanted into a mother. The mother gives birth to an organism identical to the adult that donated the nucleus.

This computer-generated image shows the way cells divide during cloning.

The first time an animal was cloned was in 1952. It was a tadpole that did not survive into adulthood. Dolly, a sheep, was cloned in 1996. She survived into adulthood and even had six healthy offspring naturally. Dolly wasn't cloned for the fun of it. Genetically changed animals, such as sheep and cows, can help us. They are capable of making human proteins in their milk that can help treat diseases, such as cystic fibrosis, a respiratory disease. If you genetically engineer one animal, you can clone it to make more.

Cloning can also help endangered species that have difficulty reproducing in zoos. In 2003, an endangered African wildcat was cloned. Scientists named the wildcat Ditteaux, as in *ditto*!

You can even have your pet cloned. A couple living in West Boca, Florida, had their Labrador named Lancelot cloned for $150,000. They named their new pet Lancelot Encore.

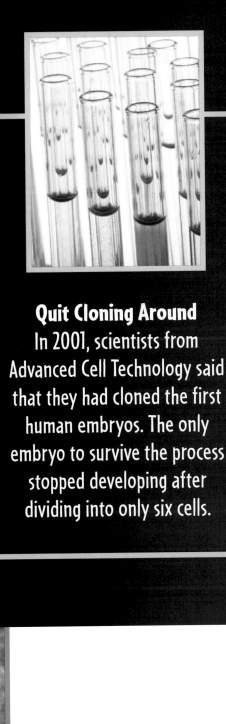

Quit Cloning Around
In 2001, scientists from Advanced Cell Technology said that they had cloned the first human embryos. The only embryo to survive the process stopped developing after dividing into only six cells.

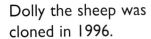

Dolly the sheep was cloned in 1996.

23

When Things Go Wrong

What happens when a genetic experiment goes wrong? According to Hollywood, you end up with a superhero like Spiderman or the Incredible Hulk.

The reality is that many genetic experiments simply flop. Before Dolly was successfully cloned, 277 attempts had failed. While many experiments have succeeded, unexpected problems have also popped up.

To increase cotton production, some cotton plants were engineered so that their leaves would repel bugs. With no leaves to eat, the caterpillars turned to the cotton flowers and ate them instead. The results—Even less cotton was produced. Caterpillars that had never eaten cotton flowers in the past changed their habits as a result of the experiment. This example shows that there are factors you cannot predict when you tinker with living things.

Mutants have been stars in science fiction for a long time.

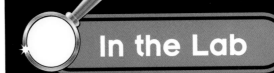

Nasty Surprises

Another example of an experiment gone wrong is the story of the soy plants. When some soy plants were genetically modified, they became so brittle they cracked open. This exposed the plants to a fungus they never would have been exposed to before.

In another experiment white petunias were engineered to be red. It worked perfectly in the lab. When released into the environment, however, the red petunias started to fade. They turned pink and even became white again. The plant had an interior battle with its new genes, and the original genes won. This natural process is called **gene silencing**. Scientists had no way of predicting the outcome of this experiment.

Silence Those Peanuts

Scientists quickly figured out that gene silencing can actually be a good thing. For example, scientists are using gene silencing to try to stop peanut allergies. They are trying to silence the gene in the peanut that causes the allergic reaction! This would make life much better for people with severe nut allergies.

Chapter 4

Same but Different

The idea of genetically modifying living things still creates fear in people. The thought of genetically modified plants and animals makes some people worry. Visions of bizarre-looking mutations form in their brains.

So what exactly does genetic modification look like? A genetically modified banana looks like, well, a banana. A genetically modified pig looks like—you guessed it—a pig. Changing the genes in an organism doesn't usually result in a change in the organism's outward appearance. In most cases, you cannot tell a genetically modified plant or animal apart from one that has not been changed. This is, perhaps, what frightens people most.

Many chickens have been genetically modified.

From chocolate to chicken, soy to salmon, genetically modified food is all around us. About 70 percent of food in the United States and Canada contains genetically modified ingredients. If you want to know what's in the food you are eating, here are a few terms that might help:

GM food—food that has been directly modified

GM ingredients—food that has ingredients that have been modified

GM ingredients in animal feed—food coming from an animal that has eaten modified food

Some countries are very strict when it comes to labeling GM foods. European countries, Japan, China, Australia, and New Zealand require GM food to be labeled. In the United States and Canada, however, GM food labeling is voluntary. Companies do not have to tell consumers that their food has been genetically modified if they don't want to!

Right now, the majority of GM crops are grown in North America. Corn and soybeans account for a good portion of genetically engineered crops.

GM Pets
Choose from neon-color GloFish™ to hypoallergenic cats. The cats are $4,000 a kitten! Or perhaps you'd prefer something sparkly for your aquarium. How about a sea horse that has the genes of a glowing jellyfish and grains of gold injected into its cells? The creature gives off light!

A Crop of Changes

Tobacco is used in cigarettes, which cause health problems. Yet tobacco has other uses. Tobacco is one of the easiest plants to change genetically. In 2008, South African scientists developed a tobacco plant that turns red when it is near a land mine. Other methods of detecting land mines are expensive and dangerous. Tobacco is a cheap alternative. Today, some companies are also trying to genetically modify tobacco plants to produce a protein that can help people with diabetes.

Tomatoes, Corn, and Potatoes

Tomatoes picked while still firm are easy to transport. Yet they do not taste as good as tomatoes that ripen on the vine. Vine-ripened tomatoes get soft fast, however, so they do not have a long shelf life in a store. In 1992, the first GM crop approved for sale to the public was the Flavr Savr. This was a tomato engineered to stay firmer longer. It was in high demand, but it never made a profit. Flavr Savr was removed from the grocery shelves.

The search for a profitable tomato that ripens right on time is still ongoing.

Corn and potatoes have been changed as well. In 1996, a gene from a bacterium that produces a type of poison was added to corn. This protects the crop from bugs such as the corn borer. A new potato might be in European fields soon.

There are two types of starch in potatoes. One type is useful in making paste, glue, and lubricants. The other type can be used to make films and foils. Both starches are good for eating. It is expensive to separate the two starches. To get around the expense, scientists are making potatoes that have only one starch.

Potatoes are being altered to separate their starches.

Popular Poplars

Genetically engineered grass and trees can help get rid of pollution. Scientists have modified poplar trees so that they can remove 91 percent of groundwater pollutants. Normal poplars can only remove three percent.

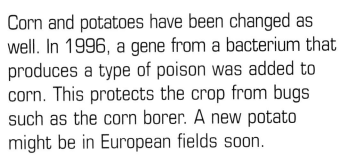

29

Amazing Animals

Transgenic animals are animals that have had the genes of another organism inserted into them. In 2006, scientists added a gene from a roundworm to a pig. The pig produced healthy omega-3 fatty acids. These fats are the same found in fish. The fats are said to have healthful benefits, as opposed to some other kinds of fats.

In 2001, Canadian researchers developed the enviropig. The enviropig's manure contains about 75 percent less phosphorus than that of typical pigs. Why do we care? Their manure is less harmful to the environment. Still other pigs have been genetically engineered to grow 40 percent faster and larger, while eating 25 percent less feed. They have been called superhogs.

Goats given spider genes produce milk that contains a useful silk.

Mighty Mice, Great Goats

Certain mice have been engineered to have no fur. Others have been engineered to run six hours without stopping. More recently, mice have been modified to show no fear of cats. The gene in charge of the instinct for fear was switched off, and the mice became real daredevils. Do we want mice like these in our houses? Of course not! Yet working with mice helps show scientists what might be possible with other animals.

Goats have had spider genes inserted into them. These goats produced spiders' silk proteins in their milk. The silk protein is called BioSteel. It is ten times stronger than steel but very flexible. It can be used for stitching in delicate medical operations. It can also be spun into a lightweight material that can be used in bulletproof vests.

Super Salmon

Typical salmon grow from an egg to a full-grown fish in about five years. Scientists have modified salmon to grow that large in about a year. These fast-growing fish might hit store shelves soon. They would be the first GM fish on your dinner table.

In the Lab

It's a Knockout

Many people's lives depend on receiving organ transplants. Scientists are working on creating "knock-out" pigs. These pigs have the genes knocked out that cause humans to reject an implanted organ. This would allow people to receive organ transplants from pigs.

Designer Child

Every cell contains the same DNA information. So what makes a skin cell different from, for example, a bone cell or a cancer cell? A gene chip is a tiny glass slide that uses thousands of neon dots to show which genes are switched on in each cell. The dots create a picture scientists can use to compare cells. By matching the light arrangement from one type of cell with that from another, you can view changes in thousands of genes at one time.

The gene chip and other advances open new possibilities. Genes are responsible for telling cells which proteins to make. If genes are not working properly, severe diseases and disorders can occur. Correcting defective genes is called gene therapy. This can include:

1. a normal gene being inserted into the genome to replace the defective gene
2. a normal gene being switched with an abnormal gene
3. an abnormal gene being repaired
4. an abnormal gene being switched off

Each baby carries DNA as unique as his or her fingerprints.

32

Some people are excited about the possibility of using gene therapy to cure diseases and disorders. Others are afraid of meddling with human life.

Doctors can fertilize an egg cell with a sperm cell outside the womb. This medical procedure has helped countless infertile couples have babies. Some people wonder if it will lead to designer babies, however. Is it okay to fill an order for a child that has a certain hair color, eye color, nose shape, height? Could we engineer talent? Personality? Intelligence? Should we? What are your thoughts on the genetic engineering of people?

On this gene chip, neon dots show which genes are "on."

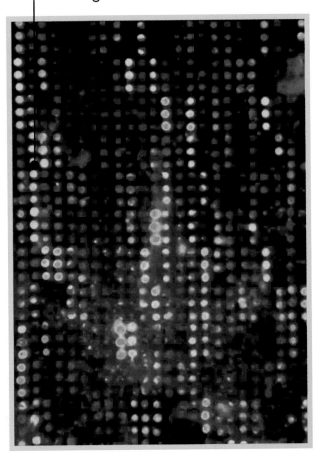

Genetic Discrimination

In the sci-fi movie *Gattaca*, children are engineered to be perfect. They are classified as *valids*. Those not genetically engineered are called *in-valids*. As part of a marketing campaign for the movie, signs were posted encouraging people to call up and have their children genetically engineered. Thousands of people called, thinking the offer was real.

33

Chapter 5

Miraculous Medicine

So where will the GM road take us? What miracles are waiting around the corner? Vaccines that are served in fruit? New cells that save lives?

Scientists have been working for some time on edible vaccines. The banana seems to be the fruit most likely to carry vaccines. Most kids like to eat bananas, the fruit can be eaten raw, and bananas grow in many developing countries. The potato has also been tested as a possible edible vaccine. Scientists have added a gene from a virus to potatoes. They have tested the potato vaccine with both mice and humans with success. To date, no edible vaccines are available to the public. Yet it is only a matter of time.

The discovery of **stem cells** is perhaps one of the most astounding of our time. These tiny cells, found in all humans, are like blanks. If the right genes are switched on and the right genes are switched off, stem cells can be turned into any type of cell in your body!

Bananas might be used as medicines.

A potato vaccine has been tested on mice.

Researchers have been able to make stem cells in the laboratory. They can use adult cells for the process. Scientists can create new blood vessels from adult bone marrow stem cells. Just imagine all the people who may be cured by having their damaged or defective cells switched with brand-new ones.

Muddy Medication

Every teaspoon of dirt contains about 10,000 different types of bacteria. Only one percent of these can be easily grown in a lab. That one percent has brought us some amazing antibiotics. What about the other 99 percent? Scientists have learned how to extract bacterial DNA from that lump of dirt. This process has already led to powerful new antibiotics.

A Hungry World

About 12 percent of the world's population is undernourished, according to the United Nations Food and Agriculture Organization. That means 854 million people need more food. Most of these people live in developing countries. The world's population is growing by six million people every year. Food prices are rising. Farmland is decreasing. The demand for food around the world is expected to increase 50 percent by the year 2030. Is the answer to our food frustrations found in genetic engineering?

Super Plants

The resurrection plant is found in South Africa. It has a gene that allows it to lose up to 95 percent of its water reserve and remain alive. Scientists found a similar gene in a plant called mouse-ear cress. The scientists modified the gene so it would kick in more often. The plant lasted 16 days without water. Food researchers hope their findings will lead to the creation of corn, wheat, and soy that can stand up to drought.

If corn used less water, it could be grown in more places around the world.

Almonds and a number of other foods from plants are high in calcium but are also high in oxalates. Oxalates stop your body from absorbing calcium. Scientists are working on modifying plants to lower the oxalates in the foods the plant produces. That way, people can absorb more calcium from what they eat.

Glossy 15 is a gene that acts like a type of sunscreen in corn. It gives young corn plants their shiny appearance. This gene is also responsible for slowing the growth rate of the plant. Scientists discovered that by doubling this gene, the corn plants grew more slowly. The corn also grew much larger.

Terminator Technology

Some seeds are engineered so that after growing, they will not produce new seeds. This forces farmers to purchase new seeds every year. It keeps the seed companies in business. What would be arguments for that practice? What would be arguments against it?

Writing in Code

Mary Shelley wrote a novel about a scientist named Frankenstein. The book came out in 1818. In Shelley's story, Dr. Frankenstein stitches together parts from dead bodies to create artificial life. Nearly two hundred years later, scientists are actually able to create artificial life. Instead of stitching together dead tissue, however, they are working on a microscopic scale.

Craig Venter is one of the DNA researchers involved in the Human Genome Project. In 2007, he stitched together laboratory chemicals to build a synthetic chromosome. It was 381 genes long and contained 580,000 base pairs. He presented it as "the creation of the first new artificial life form on Earth." The image of Venter "stitching together" new life is eerily similar to that of Dr. Frankenstein.

Craig Venter created a chromosome with a mix of lab chemicals.

Scientists have also created other artificial cell parts. They have been able to make **ribosomes**. Those are the parts in a cell where protein is manufactured. Will doctors one day be able to combine chemicals and proteins as if they were the ingredients in a cake? Will they create a completely artificial cell?

Dead Gene Comes Back to Life

About 50 million years ago, a gene that fought germs such as the tuberculosis germ was eliminated in primates. A tiny bit of that gene continued to be passed from generation to generation, however. Scientists have discovered that the dead gene has made a comeback. The gene has been found in great apes, which are related to humans.

The Future of Life

The subject of genetic engineering causes heated discussions. People seem to be either passionately for it, or passionately against it. Take a look at some of their arguments. Then decide for yourself which side of the DNA fence you are on.

Thumbs Up!

By understanding the form and function of living things, scientists are close to designing living things at will.

Humans has been genetically modifying plants and animals using selective breeding for thousands of years.

Engineering plants to resist disease will produce more food.

Genetic engineering has the potential of curing severe diseases.

Genetic engineering can help fix the world's food problems.

Genetic engineering can produce plants that are heartier, larger, and more useful.

Some GM crops are good for wildlife.

Genetically modified grass and trees can help clean the environment.

Genetically engineering pigs for organ transplants can save many lives.

No Way!

Scientists may understand the form and function of living things, but the heart of living things has to do with personality and spirit. These cannot be engineered.

Selective breeding does not cross things that would never cross naturally, such as a worm with a pig.

The gene for resistance to a virus might spread and recombine with viral information inside the plant to create new, possibly dangerous diseases.

Using viruses to deliver genes into humans could lead to making people immune to antibiotics (medicines that fight illness).

Engineered food is just another way for big companies to make more money.

Once released into the wild, GM plants cannot be controlled. In fact, GM plants have been found far from the fields where they are tested.

Some GM crops cause a reduction in wildlife.

Genetically modified plants and crops can spread their seeds, causing what some call genetic pollution.

What happens when genetically engineered animals accidentally get into the food chain?

What Do YOU Think?

Get a piece of paper and make two columns, one "for" and one "against."
How many ideas can you add?

For	Against
There are many hungry people, and anything we can do to feed them is good.	We might make monster species without realizing it.

Fabulous Pharmaceuticals

Scientists are modifying plants and animals to produce useful products. Some of these new products could become common in your lifetime. Scientists are, for example, trying to grow medicine in plants. This practice could produce drugs that are cheaper than the drugs made in labs.

We use antibodies to fight infections and even cancers. Antibodies usually come from donated blood, which is often in limited supply. To solve the problem, scientists are trying to get chickens to produce antibodies in their eggs. A chicken can lay about 330 eggs a year.

Clever Cotton and Wonderful Wheat

Researchers are creating cotton that is engineered to be blue! This would mean that your jeans would not have to be dyed. You may also be able to put your iron away forever. New cotton fibers that do not twist or wrinkle are being produced.

There is also an effort underway to make wheat that could produce biodegradable plastic wrap, cups, and plates. Wheat could also become a low-calorie fat substitute.

Earth-Friendly Fuels

Burning fossil fuels, such as petroleum, is hard on the environment. Gas and oil are not renewable sources of energy, either. Scientists are working on fuels that are both environmentally friendly and renewable.

Engineered enzymes could eventually replace harsh chemicals, such as phosphate, in detergents. This could result in detergents that do not harm the environment. Plenty of improvements are on the way.

If cotton came in colors, we would not have to dye clothes.

Take the Test!

When it comes to genetics, what seems wacky might be true. What seems reasonable may not be so. Research the following to see what is real.

1. Grapples are apples that contain grape genes.
2. Rabbits with tiger-striped fur have tiger genes.
3. Love bugs are a genetic experiment that escaped from a lab in Florida.
4. You can purchase DNA over the Internet.
5. When you eat food you are eating genes.
6. Fishberries are strawberries genetically engineered with fish genes.
7. Omega-3 eggs come from genetically modified hens.
8. The word Frankenfood is in the dictionary.
9. There is a law against genetic discrimination.

Scientists have genetically engineered a mouse with a human ear. It's true!

Answers: 1. F 2. F 3. F 4. T 5. T 6. F 7. F 8. T 9. T

Clone a Cabbage

Material:

- A head of cabbage (preferably Napa cabbage)
- Sealable plastic Baggies
- Water mister or spray bottle
- Various growing materials, such as soil, wet paper towels, compost, mulch, dead leaves
- Tray or cookie sheet

Method:

1. Pull the leaves off the cabbage until all you have is the stem. You can use the leaves for coleslaw or stir-fry.
2. With an adult's help, slice the stem into pieces about 1 inch (2.5 cm) long.
3. Half-fill each Baggie with a different type of growing material. Add a piece of cabbage stem.
4. Spray the material in the Baggie a few times until the growing material is moist, but not soaking.
5. Seal the Baggies and place them on the tray. Set the tray in sunlight near a window.
6. After one week, open the bags and examine the cabbage stem. Do you notice anything? Return each stem to its Baggie. Spray once or twice with water and reseal. Leave the tray out for another week.
7. After two to three weeks, you should see new cabbages forming. These are actually clones of the original cabbage! Are there any differences? Where on the stem are they forming? Which growing material made the best clones? Are there any materials that did not make any clones?

Now try using a celery stem, slices of carrot, or garlic!

For Further Information

Books

Allman, Toney. **Great Medical Discoveries: Stem Cells**. Farmington Hills, Mich.: Lucent Books, 2006.

McLeish, Ewan. **Genetic Revolution: A Look at the Way the World Is Today** (Issues of the World). Mankato, Minn.: Stargazer Books.

Stephenson, Frank H. **DNA: How the Biotech Revolution is Changing the Way We Fight Disease**. Amherst, N.Y.: Prometheus Books, 2007.

Web sites

www.eurekascience.com/ICanDoThat/index.htm

www.sciencedaily.com

http://tiki.oneworld.net/genetics/home.html

quote

"It is difficult to imagine a greater imposition [than adding] genes to future generations that changes the nature of future people."

Ian Wilmut

in The Second Creation: *Dolly and the Age of Biological Control*

Glossary

adenine One of the four chemical bases that make up the rungs of DNA

bacteria Type of prokaryotic organism

bases Chemicals used to make up the rungs of DNA

biolistics Technique of shooting DNA into a cell with a gene gun

cell Smallest unit that makes up every living thing

cell wall Exterior surface of prokaryotic cells and eukaryotic plant cells

chromosomes Coiled threads of DNA containing genes

clone An organism genetically identical to another

crossbreed An animal or a plant that is a mixture of two breeds within the same species

cytosine One of the four chemical bases that make up the rungs of DNA

deoxyribonucleic acid (DNA) Long strand of genetic information found in a cell's nucleus

dominant The trait that will show itself even if it is on only one chromosome

embryo A fertilized egg whose cells have started to divide

eukaryotic cells Plant and animal cells that have a nucleus

genes Sections of a chromosome that code for a certain protein

gene silencing The "switching off" of a gene

genetic engineering Changing an organism by altering, removing, or inserting genes

genome Total genetic information for an organism

guanine One of the four chemical bases that make up the rungs of DNA

Human Genome Project The mapping of all the genetic information in a human

insulin A hormone produced by the pancreas that helps control sugar in the body

mutations Change in the structure of the DNA of an organism

natural selection Process by which the organisms that best adapt to their environment survive and reproduce

nucleoid Large space inside prokaryotic cells that contains genetic material

nucleus Control center of plant or animal cells

plasma membrane Exterior surface of eukaryotic cells

plasmid A circle of DNA, separate from the chromosomes, found mainly in bacteria

prokaryotic cells Cells that do not have a nucleus

proteins Large molecules needed for the structure and function of a body's cells

recessive The trait that will show itself if the code for it is on both chromosomes

recombinant DNA A technique that changes or manipulates the DNA of a cell

ribosomes Parts of the cell that build proteins

selective breeding Choosing plants or animals to breed based on their characteristics

stem cells Cells that can develop into a variety of cell types

thymine One of the four chemical bases that make up the rungs of DNA

transgenic animals Animals that have had other DNA introduced into their own DNA

viruses Tiny organisms made mainly of protein-covered DNA able to live only on a living being

Index